CALAZAZA'S DELICIOUS DERELICTION

Tupelo Press Poetry in Translation

Abiding Places: Korea, South and North, by Ko Un
Translated from Korean by Hillel Schwartz and Sunny Jung

Invitation to a Secret Feast: Selected Poems, by Joumana Haddad
Translated from Arabic by Khaled Mattawa with Najib Awad,
Issa Boullata, Marilyn Hacker, Joumana Haddad, Henry Matthews,
and David Harsent

Night, Fish and Charlie Parker, by Phan Nhien Hao
Translated from Vietnamese by Linh Dinh

Stone Lyre: Poems of René Char
Translated from French by Nancy Naomi Carlson

This Lamentable City: Poems of Polina Barskova
Edited by Ilya Kaminsky and translated from Russian by the editor
with Katie Farris, Rachel Galvin, and Matthew Zapruder

New Cathay: Contemporary Chinese Poetry
Edited by Ming Di and translated from Chinese by the editor with Neil
Aitken, Katie Farris, Christopher Lupke, Tony Barnstone, Nick Admussen,
Jonathan Stalling, Afaa M. Weaver, Eleanor Goodman, Ao Wang, Dian Li,
Kerry Shawn Keys, Jennifer Kronovet, Elizabeth Reitzell, and Cody Reese

Ex-Voto, by Adélia Prado
Translated from Brazilian Portuguese by Ellen Doré Watson

Gossip and Metaphysics: Russian Modernist Poems and Prose
Edited by Katie Farris, Ilya Kaminsky, and Valzhyna Mort,
with translations by the editors and others

Calazaza's Delicious Dereliction, by Suzanne Dracius
Translated from French and Creole by Nancy Naomi Carlson

CALAZAZA'S DELICIOUS DERELICTION

poems by
SUZANNE DRACIUS

translated by
Nancy Naomi Carlson

T P

TUPELO PRESS
North Adams, Massachusetts

Library of Congress Cataloging-in-Publication Data

Dracius Suzanne.
  Calazaza's delicious dereliction : poems / by Suzanne Dracius ; translated
by Nancy Naomi Carlson. -- First paperback edition.
    pages cm -- (Tupelo Press poetry in translation)
  Originally published in French and Creole as Exquise déréliction métisse,
with some poems translated into English or Spanish.
  Includes bibliographical references.
  Text in English, French, and Creole.
  ISBN 978-1-936797-64-6 (pbk. : alk. paper)
1. Dracius, Suzanne--Translations into English. I. Carlson, Nancy Naomi,
1949- translator. II. Dracius, Suzanne. Poems. Selections. III. Dracius,
Suzanne. Poems. Selections. English. IV. Title.
  PQ3949.2.D73A2 2015
  841'.914--DC23

                    2015022361

Cover and text designed by Dede Cummings.
Cover art: "Woman of Martinique" (1887), by Paul Gauguin (1848–1903).
Painted terracotta (7 ¾ inches). The Henry and Rose Pearlman Collection,
on longterm loan to Princeton University Art Museum (L.1988.62.63).
Photo: Bruce M. White.
Used with permission of ArtResource (http://www.artres.com/).

First paperback edition: November 2015.

Tupelo Press
P.O. Box 1767, North Adams, Massachusetts 01247
Telephone: (413) 664–9611 / editor@tupelopress.org / www.tupelopress.org

Tupelo Press is an award-winning independent literary press that publishes
fine fiction, nonfiction, and poetry in books that are a joy to hold as well as
read. Tupelo Press is a registered 501(c)(3) nonprofit organization, and we
rely on public support to carry out our mission of publishing extraordinary
work that may be outside the realm of the large commercial publishers.
Financial donations are welcome and are tax deductible.

Supported in part by an award from the National Endowment for the Arts
and the Montgomery County Arts & Humanities Council

Aux Mânes de ma grand-mère Germaine, qui fut ma première lectrice.

— S. D.

For Miel, with love.

— N. N. C.

CONTENTS

Carmina amicitiae / Poems of Friendship

Laconique art poétique / Laconic Ars Poetica

Clausule / Clausula

PROSOPOPÉES SUBURBAINES

SUBURBAN PROSOPOPOEIA

Anamnésie propitiatoire

In extremis dans le Neuf Cube
Ce n'est pas que le 93 ni le Neuf Trois : c'est le Neuf Cube
En piles de cubes pas si neufs
Dressés
Garçon debout dans le refus de te faire dresser
Exhalant le Vicks VapoRub
Tu te rues vers quoi te référer
Intra muros
Neuf Au Carré
Jamais en odeur de sainteté
Ni en guerre contre les Gaulois
Ni contre quelque quidam que ce soit
La haine contre personne pourtant
C'est la guerre à finir toutes les guerres
Dans un bain de sang
Gnomes versus nains
La guerre à finir toutes les guerres
Résonne sous ton capuchon
À tes oreilles la chanson
Fatale « Police-menottes-prison »
La charge
Parmi les effluves incendiaires
Tandis que d'aucuns prêchent raison
En utopie du Black-Blanc-Beur
Du dedans vécue comme un leurre
S'il faut remonter aux Croisades
Y a-t-il une vie après le périf ?
Fût-ce une gageure que tu kiffes

Propitious Anamnesis

In extremis, the furthest reach in the *Neuf Cube*
Not only "the 93" nor the "Nine Three": it's the "New Cube"
In heaps of cubes not so new
High-rise
Boy standing erect, refusing to be subdued
Exuding Vicks VapoRub
You rush toward any landmarks you can trust
Intra muros, within the walls
"Nine Squared"
Never with saintly airs
Nor at war with the Gauls
Nor with some *quidam* whose name you don't know
Hate for no one
Yet it's the war to end all wars
In a bloodbath
Gnomes versus dwarves
The war to end all wars
Resounds beneath your hood
In your ears the fatal refrain
"Police-handcuffs-jail"
The charge
Among the incendiary fumes
While some preach reason
Utopian Black-White-*Beur*
From inside perceived as illusion
Going back to the time of crusades
Is there life beyond the *périf?*
Even if it was a dare you adored

Tu n'as plus pour nom prolétaire
Comme tes parents en galère.
Nul ne t'appelle contestataire
Comme ceux de Mai 68 naguère
Hors du contrôle des grands frères
Tu peux faire sans.
Le Neuf au Carré s'encanaille
Quoi que tu fasses, taxé de racaille
Où que tu ailles, pris en tenaille
« Où qu'il aille un nègre demeure un nègre »
Dixit en son temps Fanon.
Tu as envie d'apprendre à dire non.

Chabin de toute façon tu es mal.
Pour faire « négro » tu as le teint trop pâle
Il n'y a que ta carte qui fasse sefran
Pour le reste ni assez dark ni assez blanc
Tu as plus l'air maghrébin que noir
Tu n'as jamais la bonne couleur
Pour ton malheur
Te voilà estampillé canaille
Rebeu ou beur
Plus tu es de couleur
Moins tu es visible
À chaque contrôle on te tutoie
Te traite comme un chien, te rudoie
Dès que tu vois babylone, tu cours
Tu as une trop bonne tête à bavure
Nul besoin de prouver ta bravoure
Gare, si tu ralentis l'allure
Éperdu, hagard, tu percutes
Pour toi, plus dure sera la chute
Pour peu que tu te trouves au pied du mur
Si tu sautes, tu t'électrocutes
Sauve qui peut, c'est une histoire
Qui peut se terminer à coups de pied

"Proletarian" not your name
Like your forebears, galley slaves.
None call you "angry young man"
Like those not long ago in May '68
Out of older brothers' control
You can do it on your own.
The "Nine Squared" mixes with riffraff
Whatever you do, accused of being trash
Wherever you go, held back in a pincer's grasp
"Wherever he goes a Negro remains a Negro"
Dixit Fanon in his day.
No is what you want to learn to say.

Chabin, you are wrong at any rate.
To look "black" your face is too pale
There's only your ID card that makes you *sefran*
Otherwise not quite dark not quite white
You seem more Maghrebi than black
Your color is never right
Your bad luck
To be branded as "up to no good."
Rebeu or *beur*
The more intense your color
The less you are seen
At each check they use familiar forms of address
Bully you, treat you like a dog
As soon as babylon comes in view, you race away
Yours is a face that triggers blunders by cops
No need to prove your prowess
Look out, if you slacken your pace
Distracted, haggard, you'll crash
For you, the fall more harsh
If you find yourself with your back to the wall
If you leap, you might die from electric shock
Run for your life, it's a tale
That could end with kicks

Sous l'objectif, furtif voyeur
Très subjectivement mateur
D'une vidéo amateur.
Un gigantesque pourrissoir
Qui dégénère en bourbier,
Abracadabrantesque mouroir
Qui risque de finir en charnier
C'est la guerre à finir toutes les guerres
Dans un bain de sang
La guerre à interdire le rap
Prends garde que l'on ne t'attrape

Fille, antan on t'a cantonnée
Derrière un métier à tisser,
De nuits de veille en nuitées
D'ores et déjà il va te falloir veiller
Au métier à métisser
Dans la guerre à finir toutes les guerres
N'importe comment.
Hors des cités de maudition
Hors des barres de perdition
Métissage et marronnage
S'érigent
Émergent
Les deux mamelles de l'enfance
Métissage, moderne marronnage
Seule mammoplastie de l'En-France
Exutoire
Fort
Propitiatoire.
Fille, à force tu te dévoileras
Dès lors, ce vingt-et-unième siècle sera féminin ou ne sera pas.

In the objective lens, furtive voyeur
Very subjectively spy
Of a home video.
A gigantic compost pile
That rots into quagmire,
Abracadabra! An old folks home
That might end up a mass grave
It's the war to end all wars
In a bloodbath
The war to ban rap
Take care not to get grabbed

Girl, you were confined in bygone days
Behind a weaving loom,
Night after night wide awake
Henceforth you will have to keep watch
On the métier of *métisser*
In the war to end all wars
No matter the way.
Beyond cities under a curse
Beyond housing projects eternally damned
Métissage and *marronnage*
May they raise themselves high
Emerge
Infancy's two teats
Métissage, modern *marronnage*
The only mammoplasty of In-France
Catharsis
Courageous
Propitious.
Girl, your strength will end up revealed
From then on, this twenty-first century will be for women or
will not be.

Subnigra sum sed formosa

Te susurrerai-je en douceur que le cafard
N'a pas droit de cité sur ces bords,
Que, furtif, le *ravet* se faufile
En ces touffeurs enténébrées ?
Tu ne peux pas avoir le cafard,
Tu ne peux avoir que le ravet.
Puisses-tu, s'il te tient, le tenir,
D'une semelle leste l'écraser :
Tu prends une odeur de whisky — remugles de mauvais alcool
Ni Black Label ni Red Label ni noble bourbon.

Fors le traumatisme d'abandon,
Le non-regard,
L'oubli de ton nom
— Ni label *black* ni aristocratique Bourbon avec un B
majuscule —,
La preste déréliction émergeant de cette piètre eau-de-vie
Aux nauséabonds effluves de musc et de ravet pilé,
De cafard écrabouillé,
De cancrelat écrasé,
De blatte éventrée, étripée,
En être que l'on n'a pas reconnu
Tu ne te reconnais pas non plus.
Mais tu ne peux avoir le cafard,
Tu ne peux avoir qu'un ravet caribéen
ou une québécoise coquerelle
en kafkaïenne métamorphose.

Subnigra sum sed formosa

Will I whisper gently that the cockroach
Has no place on these shores,
That stealthy, the "ravet" weaves
In and out of this shadowed sweltering heat?
You can't get the blues.
You can only get the reggae-blues.
If it holds you, may you hold it,
Mash it with a nimble sole:
You smell whiskey — stale odor of bad alcohol,
Neither Black Label nor Red Label nor noble bourbon.

Except for the trauma of neglect,
Lack of eye contact,
Forgetting your name —
Neither "black" label nor aristocratic Bourbon with a capital "B" —
The prompt dereliction rising up from this paltry eau-de-vie
With sickening smell of musk and crushed "ravet,"
Squashed cockroach,
Crunched waterbug,
Gutted and gored cucaracha,
A being who couldn't be recognized,
You don't even recognize yourself.
But you can't get the blues,
You can only get the Caribbean blues
Or the blues from Quebec —
Metamorphosis that's Kafkaesque.

Monte, incantatoire, ta complainte :
Nigra sum sed formosa.
« Je suis noire, mais belle », dixit la Reine de Saba.
Quid de qui n'est que *subnigra* ?
Qu'y a-t-il en-dessous de *nigra* ?
Tu quémandes le regard de l'Autre
— Mais de quel Autre, au demeurant ? —
Pour appréhender que tu existes,
Piler le ravet d'un pied ferme,
Piler le ravet jusqu'au terme,
En ton métissage avancer.
Que monte, ô victoire, ton cantique :
Subnigra sum sed formosa.

Incantatory, your lament ascends:
Nigra sum sed formosa.
"I am black, but beautiful," *dixit* the Queen of Sheba.
What about those who are only *subnigra?*
What is there below *nigra?*
You beg for respect from the Other —
But which Other, for all that? —
To comprehend that you exist,
Crush the "ravet" with resolve,
Crush the "ravet" to the end,
Affirm your mixed descent.
O victory, let your song of songs ascend:
Subnigra sum sed formosa.

Pointe-des-Nègres

*à Aimé Césaire, cette prosopopée de la ville
qui eut pour maire un poète*

Là débarquèrent
naguère
les frères
et sœurs d'Afrique
en souffrance
sous France
sous-France
déportés.
Là s'épand ma gésine urbaine.
Thalassique est cette hystérie :
ce ventre est ventre
de la mer.
J'ai fécondé l'écume marine.
Moi je pénètre, tendue,
la houle porteuse de négriers.
Moi j'ai pointé mon phallus
dans l'utérus
océan
pour en faire naître des lots de nègres
tout debout.
D'ores et déjà, désormais
je fais assaut d'urbanité
sans parvenir à oublier
que je me nomme « Pointe-des-Nègres »
dépossédée de mon nom d'Afrique.

Pointe-des-Nègres

to Aimé Césaire (1913–2008),
this prosopopoeia of the town who had a poet as mayor

Here came ashore
some time ago
brothers
and sisters from Africa
on sufferance
under France
sub-France
expelled.
Here my urban birthing pours forth.
This rapture is thalassic:
this womb is the womb
of the sea.
I've impregnated maritime froth.
I penetrate, stiff,
the swell bearing ships of slaves.
I've driven my phallus
into the uterus
of ocean
causing Negroes in lots to be born
all erect.
Here and now, for all time ahead
I mount an attack on urbanity
striving in vain to forget
that I am named *Pointe-des-Nègres*
deprived of my African name.

Comment me crièrent-ils
antan
ces enchaînés, lorsqu'ils posèrent
sur mon écale
leurs millions de pieds sanguinolents :
Fongo ? *Dankan* ? *Goanuà* ?
Ou bien *Nchi Kavu* ou *Goà* ?

Montent à mon oreille par gros vent
les noms qu'ils me hurlèrent naguère
ces rauques gosiers africains
avant que je ne fusse « Pointe-des-Nègres »,
pendant que j'étais *Pointe à Nègres*,
pendant que, de mon fer pointé
au fond des entrailles de la mer,
naissaient des lots, des piles de nègres
à l'envi,
des charges de nègres
à l'encan,
de mes graines, dans l'effervescence
de la matrice océane
au temps où je violais, impavide,
l'immensité caraïbe.
En elle j'épandis ma semence
en plein mitan de cet océanique bassin.
En sortirent des myriades de nègres
debout,
hauts congos,
haut levés.

Quel nom d'Afrique me donnèrent-ils
avant que les leucodermes
ne me baillent pour nom « Pointe-des-Nègres » ?
Souf ? *Terrou-bi* ? *Lessdi* ?
De leurs cabèches esclavées,
de leurs boudins

How they cried out to me
long ago
those in chains, when they placed
on my bedrock
their millions of bleeding feet:
Fongo? Dankan? Goanuà?
Or *Nchi Kavu* or *Goà?*

A heavy wind brings up to my ear
the names they wailed at me in the past
those ragged African throats
before I was *Pointe-des-Nègres,*
while I was *Pointe-à-Nègres,*
while, from my rod driven
deep in the depths of the sea,
Negroes in lots, in piles were born
over and over again,
cargoes of Negroes
for the auction block,
from my seed in the fizz
of the ocean's womb
when I raped, without shame,
the immense Caribbean expanse.
In her I spread my sperm
right in the midst of that ocean basin.
From there myriad Negroes emerged
erect,
tall African brothers and sisters,
heads held high.

What African name did they give me
before the Whites
gave me the name of *Pointe-des-Nègres?*
Souf? Terrou-bi? Lessdi?
From their enslaved heads,
from their bellies

gonflés de faim,
leurs langues asséchées d'eau saline,
du tréfonds de leurs gosiers rauquis
de tant et tant crier famine,
quel nom d'Afrique pouvait sourdre ?
Fus-je criée *Mabélé*, *Oto*,
Monkili, *Hmsé* ou *Molongo* ?
Lorsque, sur ma squame courbant
leurs indénombrables échines
lacérées à coups de chicotte,
ils posèrent leurs pieds en sang
couverts de chiques,
tchip ! comment avaient-ils rauqué
« Terre ! Terre ! » en leurs langues d'Afrique ?

> Terre je suis, sacrée, suburbaine,
> multicolore, à ce jour.
> En mon hypermarchand rond-point
> quelle noire lumière diffuse mon phare ?

bloated from lack of food,
their tongues parched from salt water,
from the depths of their ragged throats
so much they had cried out in hunger,
what African word could take shape?
Was I called *Mabélé, Oto,*
Monkili, Hmsé or *Molongo*?
When, on my horny hide
their countless backbones bent
cut by the lash of the whip,
they planted their bloodied feet
covered with chiggers,
tchip! how did they hoarsely shout
"Land! Land!" in their African tongues?
                    Land that I am, sacred, suburban,
                        multicolored, to this day.
                In my hypermarket roundabout
            what black light diffuses my lighthouse's beam?

Terres-Sainville

Brandir le nom d'Amédée Knight
Le premier sénateur noir
En oriflamme
Et exalter langue créole
Là
En langue française materner
Exhausser harmonies créoles
En marinades
Pimentées d'hellènes latinades
Natale faire offrande du fondòk
Et du fondal-natal faire don
Enseigner à fervente marmaille
Manière de lire le monde en moi
Natale lui apprendre comment
Écrire le monde à partir
De mon dédale de venelles
Humble matrice d'érudition

Pour un peu j'étais à Castries
Je lui aurais baillé de l'anglais
Tchip ! je suis foyalaise en diable
J'ai failli être dominicaine
On peut me traiter de schizophrène
Nous sommes plusieurs :
Terres Sainville

Ruelles créoles délicieusement
Peuplées de maisonnettes créoles

Terres-Sainville

Let's brandish the name of Amédée Knight
First black senator
As a banner
And extol the Creole tongue
Over there
In the French tongue, cradle and rock
Enhance Creole harmonies
In marinades
Spiced with hellenic *latinades*
From birth make an oblation: secret depths, the *fondòk*
And from the fundamental, a gift
To teach eager boys and girls
The way to read the world in me
From birth show them how
To write the world
From my labyrinth of alleys
Humble matrix of knowledge

I nearly was in Castries
I would have given them English
Tchip! I was born and bred in Fort-de-France
I almost was Dominican
They can treat me like a schizophrenic
Several we are:
Sainville lands

Creole back streets deliciously
Filled with Creole gingerbread cottages

En pain d'épices de dentelle de bois en frises et festons
De populations créoles
De tout partout
Que pour l'heure on réhabilite
Tandis que tout long cohabitent
Salsa du démon de la chair
Et pis
Prêchi-prédicateurs en chaire
Et pis
Replètes filles de joie hispaniques
Et pis et pis
La békée-goyave nostalgique
Le déménageur débonnaire
Qui un soir sortit son fusil pour ouvrir la chasse
Aux maquereaux
La Haïtienne bonne à tout faire
Et pis
Contre vents et marées
La harengère qui végète
En sa poissonnerie qui surnage
En sa boutique
Tel un radeau
Se débat contre
L'hyper tératologique
Et pis
Et pis
L'indestructible comptoir de Chin

Marécage nous étions naguère
À l'heure où
Rescapés de Saint-Pierre
AtTERRirent
Noirs et mulâtres
En bas feuilles
Sur le marigot asséché du sieur Sainville où je gis
Vie trépidante

Lacy with friezes and garlands carved out of wood
Filled with Creole people
From everywhere and beyond
Houses that nowadays they restore
While coexisting one and all
Salsa from the devil of the flesh
And then
Preachy preachers on pulpits
And then
Plump Hispanic *filles de joie*
And also and then
The nostalgic *békée-goyave*, white Creole woman flat broke
The mild-mannered furniture mover
Who took out his gun one night to pursue
The pimps
The Haitian maid who goes all the way
And then
Against all odds
The fishmonger, worn down
In her fish store that barely stays afloat
In her shop
Hanging on, as if to a raft
Struggling against
The monstrous hypermarket
And then
And then
Chin's indestructible counter

We were swamp not long ago
At the time when
Survivors from Saint-Pierre
LANDed
Mulattos and blacks
Down in the leaves
On mister Sainville's drained marshland where I lie
Hectic life

Aux sans-logis pierrotins catastrophés
Havre de grâce effervescente

Rôde encore le chômeur *zorey*
C'est moins pénible au soleil
Tandis que s'envolent au loin
Les natives-natales
Qui s'en vont
Peupler d'autres banlieues, là-bas
Sur l'Autre Bord
Y a-t-il une vie
Après le périphérique ?

Han han ! Nulle flambée de colère
Ni nulle ardeur délétère
Ça bout de ferveurs tropicales
En d'improbables hivers
Conjurant toute déréliction
Sans spéculer sur d'autres mondes
En dignité suburbaine
Si mystique et tellement humaine
Terrienne
Hissant haut toponyme
En tripartite tellurisme
D'hystérie sacrée, souveraine
En toute modestie hautaine
Résolument excentrique
Portant
Terres
Saint
Ville
En mon nom
Et portant beau

For the devastated homeless from Saint-Pierre
Haven of effervescent grace

The out-of-work *zorey* still wanders about
It's less of a hardship in sun
While natal-natives
Take off for distant lands
Leaving
To populate other outskirts, there
On the Other Shore
Is there a life
Beyond the peripheral?

Han han! No! No! No blazes of rage
Nor baleful zeal
It seethes with tropical fires
In improbable winters
Warding off all dereliction
Without speculation about other worlds
In suburban dignity
So mystic, so human
Terrestrial
Hoisting a toponyme high
In tripartite tellurism
With hysteria, sacred, supreme
In full modesty, sublime
Staunchly excentric
Bearing
Lands
Saint
Town
In my name
And looking good

VENI, VIDI, VIXI

I CAME, I SAW, I LIVED

Aux horizons du Sud

Couleur, chaleur et mêmes odeurs
Nous avons tous cela au cœur
Hors des sillons de certitude
Nous autres, aux horizons du Sud

Cadence et danse, indépendance
Ne pas retomber en enfance
Ne pas voir misère en En-France
En la Troisième Île : Île-de-France
Hors des traces de servitude
Insulaires esseulés
Et seuls
Et seules
Nous autres, aux horizons du Sud

Nos brumes sont de sable, de chaleur
Nos signes, Tropiques ou Equateur
Enfants de la mer
Filles de sable
À peau noire
D'origine arabe

Par-delà mangrove et savane
Enchaînés à
Métropolis
Envoûtés par
Mégapolis
Vent-menés par Traite et trafic

In Southern Horizons

Color, same odors, and heat
We all hold them in our hearts
Except for furrows of certitude
All of us, in southern horizons

Independence, cadence and dance
Let's not regress to infancy
Let's not see distress in In-France
In the Third Island: Île-de-France
Except for shadows of servitude
Islanders isolated
Men alone
Women alone
All of us, in southern horizons

Our mists are of sand, our signs
Of heat, Equatorial or Tropic
Children of the sea
Girls of sand
With black skin
Of Arab descent

Beyond savanna and mangrove swamp
Shackled to
Metropolis
Bewitched by
Megalopolis
Windswept by slave trade and traffic

Venus des horizons du Sud

Quimboisés par toutes leurs polices
Leurs leucodermes démonades
Vaudou sur nous !
En débandade, ire ou dérade
Aliénés par toutes ces peaux lisses
Et cheveux droits comme il se doit
Au pays des Droits de l'Homme
Quimbois, vaudou !
Tiens, bois, doudou !
Aliénés par ces cheveux qui glissent
Masques blancs sans
Ces peaux sauvées
Chevelures grainées
Mêlés nos sangs
D'échappés
Banania, bamboula, macaque
Diaspora Black
Nous avons des passés qui marquent
Et aussi un présent qui claque
Un passé de marques
Gens de marque
Au nez et aux barbes barbares
De nazillons nasillards

Pour s'ouvrir l'avenir se démarque
Prendre nos marques
À vos marques
Prêts
Partez
Nous courons vite, longtemps et loin
Jamaïcains ou Éthiopiens
Droit devant
Sans drapeau, au vent
D'Îles au Vent

Arrived from southern horizons

Spirits possessed by all their police
Their black magic with white skin
Voodoo on us!
In stampede, ire or erratic ways
Alienated by those with smoother skin
And straight hair fixed right
In the land of the Rights of Man
Quimbois, voodoo!
Take this, drink, my dear!
Alienated by hair like silk
White masks without
This rescued skin
Frizzy hair
Our blood mixed
With those who escaped
Banania, bamboula, macaque
Black Diaspora
We have pasts that leave a mark
And also a present that clacks
A past of marks
People of mark
Thumbing their nose
At nasal neo-nazis and barbaric beards

To open, the future eludes its marker
Take our marks
On your mark
Get set
Go
We run fast, a long time and far
Jamaicans or Ethiopians
Straight ahead
Without flag, in the wind
Of Windward Islands

Sans hymnes, au vent d'Îles sous le Vent
Soulevant
Haut nos fronts bistres
Sangs-mêlés
Sans-papiers, sans dieux ni maîtres
Sans chemise
Sans pantalon
Sans papiers
Sans-papiers
Sans maître
Sans foi
Ni loi
Délits de faciès
Bavures pour babylones barbares
Nous autres, aux arcs-en-morne du Sud

Griffe, sacatra, capre, capresse, signare, griffonne
Négritte, négrille, négrillonne
Octavon, congo, quarteronne, mamelouque, marabou, métif,
métive...

Marron, marronne !

Blanche-Neige, basané, métèque
Bougnoule — « noir » en wolof, « arabe » en argot féroce —
Des mots qui nous font des bosses
Des maux qui nous donneront force
D'être bien debout dans nos peaux
Nous autres, aux arcs-en-ciel du Sud
Boule-de-neige, sang-mêlé, négro
Des mots qui font de nous des zéros
Des maux qui font de nous des héros
Des mots qui feront de nous des hérauts
Bronzé, mal lavé, moricaud
Négro, négresse à plateau
Mal blanchi, café au lait

Without hymns, in the wind of Leeward Islands
Lifting
High our swarthy brows
People of mixed descent
Illegal immigrants, sans masters or gods
Sans shirt
Sans pants
Sans documents
Illegal immigrants
Sans master
Sans trust
Nor law
Condemned for the wrong color of skin
Fodder for blunders by barbaric Babylones
All of us, in southern rainbow hills

Griffe, sacatra, cascos, sambo, mango
Mustifee, mustifino
Octoroon, congo, quadroon, meamelouc, marabon, metif . . .

Maroon men, Maroon women!

Snow White, bronzed, metic
Bougnoule — "Black" in Wolof, "Arab" in savage slang —

Words that wound us
Wrongs that will give us strength
To stand tall in our skin
All of us, in southern rainbows
Snowball, mixed blood, negro
Words that make us zeroes
Wrongs that make us heroes
Tanned, dirty, dark
Negro, Negress with Mursi plate lips
Badly whitened, café au lait
Negrita rum, swarthy and flashy foreigner

Négrita, bistre et rastaquouère
Bique, bicot, crouille, melon, beur
Raton, keubla, gens de couleur
Et si nous avions dans la tête
De nous sentir bien dans nos peaux
Nous autres, aux horizons du Sud ?

Bique, bicot, crouille, melon, beur
Dirty rat, *keubla*, colored
And if we had in our head
To feel good in our skin
All of us, in southern horizons?

Moun le Sid

(Creole)

Koulè, chalè èk menm lodè
Nou tout ni zafè-a an tjè.
Annou sòti an wèt ki ja sav
Pwan chimen chyen
Las tiré dlo an penyen
Nou menm la, sé moun le Sid.

Kadans èk dans, Lendépendans
Fòk pa ritonbé an anfans
Fòk pa pran fè an Anfrans !
Annou sòti an vyé tras lèsklavaj
Annou chapé mawon an vyé tras lestravay
Nou menm la, manmay le Sid.

Siren kay nou, sé sab épi chalè
Sin nou, Twopik oben Lekwatè.
Ti manmay lanmè, ti moun sab
Sa ki nwè oben ki arab
Pli lwen pasé mangròv, savann
Anba jouk Métwopolis
Maré adan Mégapolis
Maré ren-nou
Sòti kò-nou an ladévenn
Tiré san-nou an ladévenn
Yo di ki koko ni dlo, zabriko ni grenn :
Tout moun sòti an Sid latè-a.

Kaf èk kongo èk makak
Ba nou, an tan lontan, sé mak
Épi jòdi jou, an fwi rak
Ba nou menm la, moun le Sid.
Dépi matji Danten i bout.
Ki moun atjòlman ké di hak ?
Sa ki fondòk, sa ki ti kréyòl tjòlòlò
Vanmennen, déchouké, mawon !
Pawòl ka fè nou anpil bòs.
Aprézan fòk nou ni lafòs
Rété doubout an lapo-nou
Lévé doubout an koulè-nou
Nou tout la ki fèt le Sid.

Milat, chapé, tout manmay nèg
Dé vyé ti mo, kat vyé pawòl
Ki fè nou zéwo douvan chif
Tèt koko sèk, chaben pwèl si
Oben chaben blèm blèm tou
Pwél mangous, dé kout tanbou
Batasiryen, batakouli
Chapé kouli, nwè kon an kaka kochon
Nwè kon an kaka démon
Kouli manjé chyen, malaba
Nèg gwo siwo, batachinwa
Prèlè ki kon an eskwaya
Milat-négrès pa manman-y
Kalazaza, wayayay
Gwo nèg, kalvè
Chonjé pawòl an bouch pa chay !
Asé chayé makrélaj !
Annou katjilé an tèt-nou
Sé byen nou byen an lapo nou
Nou tout la ki sé moun le Sid

L'entrebâillement de la porte

à Samantha et à Marie Gauthier

En plénitude d'œil ouvert,
Polychroïsme jouant dans
L'entrebâillement de la porte
Au gré de ces incidences que, vive, la lumière apporte
En multitude, champ offert
Par surgissement d'incarnats
Sur fleurs épandues en émoi
D'infinitude d'yeux cillant,
Immuable regard vigilant
Sur l'insigne féminitude,
Ton avenir n'est pas si différent du mien ;
Pourtant nos passés abolis divergent bien.
Or dans l'entrebâillement de la porte, là,
Paraît ton présent, Pandora.
Car dans l'entrebâillement furtif de la porte, là,
L'Espérance au fond restera.
Si s'oblitérait le passé, nous serions tous condamnés
À mille fois le ressasser.
Sur tréfonds d'ardent nacarat,
De sueurs, de sucres et de sangs,
Mêlés — ô métissage fervent —
Absolu regard vigilant,
Dresse-toi, libre, tu es là,
Fière, affranchie, Pandora.
Marronne de corps et de cœur,
Marron de force et de couleur,

The Gap of the Cracked-Open Door

for Samantha and for Marie Gauthier

In vision's plenitude, open eye's gaze,
Pleochroic crystals at play
In the gap of the cracked-open door
At the will of these angles of incidence brought by myriad rays
Of bright light, a multitude, field bestowed
By sudden profusions of flesh-colored tones
Of flowers, aroused, pouring forth
With limitless blinking eyes,
Immutable vigilant watch
Over grand *feminitude*,
Your future's not far from mine;
However, suppressed, our pasts still greatly diverge.
Now in the gap of the cracked-open door, here,
Pandora, your present appears.
For in the furtive gap of the cracked-open door, here,
In the back, Hope will endure.
If the past were to cancel itself, we'd all be doomed
To review it a thousand times in our heads.
On depths of glowing and nacreous orange-red hues,
Sweats, sugars, and bloods,
Blended—O fervent *métissage*—
Keep absolute vigilant watch,
Stand up straight, free, you are here,
Emancipated, proud, Pandora.
Maroon in body and heart,
Maroon in color and might,

Pour marronner, faire le mur,
Fuir, altièrement fugueuse.
Les murs de la honte, fougueuse,
Les dirimer, trouver la faille.
La dive porte s'entrebâille :
Sans procrastiner, Pandora,
Sur tréfonds de vif baccarat,
Cristal torturé par de volcaniques ardeurs,
Laisse gloser ces fronts d'exégètes factices
Sur les indécryptables essences métisses.
Abandonne-leur ces pâleurs,
Ce qu'ils érigent en valeurs.
Quitte-les, ces pisse-copie !
D'Afrique et d'Inde et d'Utopie,
Dans l'entrebâillement de la porte, là,
Paraît ton présent, Pandora.
Parée pour ta Révolution,
Telle une ultime Abolition,
Parée, oui, de tous les dons,
Femme debout sur fleurs haut levées,
Écarlates, écartelées,
Bien plantée, fermement campée
Dans la confusion de tes sangs.

To escape, climb over the wall,
Flee, noble runaway girl.
With zeal, tear down the walls of shame,
Find the flaw.
The divine door opens a crack:
Pandora, without holding back,
On depths of vivid Baccarat,
Crystal tormented by lashing waves of volcanic heat,
Let these brows of fake exegetes gloss
On the cryptic core of *métissage*.
Relieve them of their pallors,
What they hold in high esteem.
Leave them, these hacks!
From Africa, India, Utopia,
In the gap of the cracked-open door, here,
Pandora, your present appears.
Prepared for your Revolution,
Such an ultimate Abolition,
Adorned, yes, with all the gifts,
Woman standing on high-born blooms
Of scarlet, ripped to shreds,
Well-planted, firmly entrenched
In the mix of your bloods.

Antonomase en temps de cyclone

Avec les flots bruissants de la rivière qui coule au fond de ce
jardin,
S'échappant, marronnant, fluette mais fougueuse tellement
Jusqu'à la Pointe-des-Nègres — qui sait ? elle en a
l'impétuosité —
Exit la lycéenne scéenne en DS 21,
Femme pourfendue à la merci du moindre macho venu.
Existe, dans les tourbillons, les ondes bénéfiques, cycloniques
d'un vociférant *hurricane*,
Mordillé des dévorations d'érotomanes distingués,
Un palindrome salvateur de l'épéen guerrier de l'Iliade,
Le paradoxal pseudonyme si incroyablement gaulois,
En anagramme de cet homérique hapax.

Exit la moitié de moitié,
La mi-ceci mi-cela.
Existe la réappropriation d'un être dans son intégrité
— Sa totalité recouvrée,
Son entièreté assumée —
Pour qui toute discrimination positive est un oxymore,
Pour qui chaque récrimination légitime est tautologie,
Pour qui l'affirmative action n'est pas que figure de style
Pour qui le chiasme n'est pas qu'impure ou vaine rhétorique
S'il est « peau noire, blanc dedans »
Ou « la peau sauvée, noir au fond ».
Entonnant en ces temps de cyclone
Une antonomase plus réelle qu'Hercule, Apollon ou Vénus

Antonomasia in Cyclone Times

With the river's murmuring streams that flow in this garden's
   depths,
Running away, a Maroon, slight but so spirited
Reaching Pointe-des-Nègres — who knows? — out of control —
Exit the schoolgirl from Sceaux in DS 21,
Woman slain at the mercy of even the lowliest macho who came.
There exists, in whirlpools, in propitious and swirly waves of a
   raging hurricane,
Nibbled but not devoured by well-bred erotomaniacs
A redeeming palindrome found in the Iliad's Epean warrior's
   name,
Paradoxical pseudonym so incredibly French,
Anagram of that hapax from Homer.

Exit the half of half,
The part-this, part-that.
There exists a person's reclaiming of self —
Her wholeness regained,
Her entirety assumed —
For whom all positive discrimination is an oxymoron,
For whom each legitimate recrimination is tautology,
For whom affirmative action is not only a figure of speech,
For whom chiasmus is not only rhetoric, vain or impure
If "black skin, white inside"
Or "saved skin, black deep down."
Intoning in these cyclone times
An antonomasia truer than Hercules, Apollo or Venus —

— Métis, métis —,
D'une palinodie plus qu'humaine,
Trois petits tours firent les Pléiades,
D'onyx et d'albâtre, puis s'en furent,
Au nombre de sept, toujours.

Metis, mestizo —
From a palinode more than human,
The Pleiades made three little turns,
Onyx and alabaster, then took off,
Still seven in all.

Finiséculaire haruspice

On dirait que des ciels s'entrouvrent,
Non encore étales, pourtant,
Somptueusement neufs, au demeurant
Et sereins, potentiellement,
Si finiséculaires, si fastes,
Si finimillénairement festifs
Pour de dextres envolées, de favorables auspices,
De multiples surgissements propices
Hors des présages funestes.

J'optai pour que tous les ciels s'ouvrent, vastes
Et clairs, en nonante-sept.
Que calme et cirée s'offre à nous l'immensité océane
— *Kalmisiré*, pour de vrai —
En nous, pour nous et alentour, *ad vitam aeternam*.

Haruspicy at Century's End

It looks like skies are opening halfway,
Not yet quiet, none the less
Lavishly new besides,
And serene, potentially,
So fin-de-siècle, so filled with luck,
So fin-de-millennium festive
For favorable flights of birds, auspicious signs,
Many propitious sightings,
Not portents of death.

I opted for all skies to open up, vast
And clear, in ninety-seven.
Let the ocean's expanse before us be calm and waxed—
Kalmisiré, for real —
In us, for us and all around, *ad vitam aeternam.*

ᖆᖆᖆᖆᖆ

ENTRE MONT PELÉ ET
MONT DE VÉNUS

BETWEEN MOUNT PELÉE
AND MOUND OF VENUS

Fantasmes de femmes

à Susanne Rinne

Il me plaît de chevaucher aussi
comme sur les fresques de Pompéi
à la Romaine, à l'Andromaque.
Alors vous porteriez ma marque
plus suave que marquage au fer rouge
d'exquise servitude abolie.
Pour une femme aussi, grand plaisir !
Ainsi n'aurez-vous rien à redire.
C'est comme ça que vous serez comblé
à faire toutes ces choses que vous dites
au coq chantant, au pipirit,
à l'infini,
toutes ces choses interdites
en théorie
comme on dit :
fantasme de femme,
en fantastique chevauchée
de haute guerrière, d'Amazone du Dahomey,
telle une fougueuse Penthésilée.

Après tout, qu'est-ce que l'on risque
à faire ces choses que vous me dites
— si d'aventure nous le faisions —
pourvu que nous le fassions
en douce folie ?

Women's Fantasies

for Susanne Rinne

It pleases me to straddle a horse and ride
like women do in the frescos of Pompeii
in the Roman way, the Andromache way.
Then you would bear my mark
sweeter than brands made
from the red iron of lovely servitude, now banned.
Great joy for a woman as well!
You'll have no cause for complaint.
You'll be sated
doing all these things you say
to the gray kingbird, to the singing cock,
without end,
all these forbidden things
in theory
as they say:
a woman's fantasy,
fantastic ride
of mighty Amazon warriors, female soldiers of Dahomey,
like Penthesilea, spirited queen.

After all, what's the danger
in doing these things that you say —
if by chance we should do them —
as long as we do them
while wildly insane?

Car une femme debout d'aujourd'hui
ne sera pas pour autant maudite.

Oh, comprenez combien j'hésite !
Mais quelle est cette pudeur dite
féminine
qui me retient aux abords ?
Je sais bien qu'il faut que j'évite
de faire ces choses que vous me dites
en malappris,
en malfini. . .
Croyez bien que cela m'irrite
que ce soient choses interdites.

Maintenant c'est moi qui vous invite
en mélodie,
en harmonie.
Faut-il vraiment que l'on soit ivre
pour faire exulter nos chairs vives ?
Faut-il que longuement l'on dérive
en féerie,
en barbarie,
extrêmes dans nos emportements
autant que dans nos engouements,
en frénésie,
en malcadi ?

Ah ! Pouvoir chevaucher aussi
comme sur les fresques de Pompéi
à l'Andromaque, à la Romaine,
ma fière monture enfourchant
à la rue d'Enfer à Saint-Pierre
juste au-dessous du volcan
sous la Pelée rue Monte au ciel,
faire toutes ces choses interdites

For an upright woman today
will not, for all that, be defamed.

Oh understand how I waver!
What is this feminine sense
of decency, its tight reins?
I'm well aware I must refrain
from doing these things you say
ill-bred,
ill-fated . . .
Believe me, I am dismayed
that these are forbidden things.

Now it is I inviting you
in melody,
in harmony.
Must we really be drunk to make
our living flesh rejoice?
Must we slowly drift away
in fairy tales,
in barbaric ways,
extreme in our rage
as in our cravings,
crazed,
convulsed?

Ah, to be able to ride
like women do in the frescos of Pompeii
like Andromache, in the Roman way,
straddling my proud horse
to Hell's Road in Saint-Pierre
just below the volcano, Rise-to-Heaven Street
under Mount Pelée,
doing all these forbidden things
in paradise,

en paradis,
m'offrir toutes ces poses que vous dites
en mystique cri,
Yé misticri !
M'offrir toutes ces poses interdites
et cric et crac
et cric crac.
Non, la cour ne va pas dormir
encore à *corps* et à cris
en hédoniste poésie,
Philosophie,
la Philo !
J'ai pris l'envol
et pis j'ai pris
courir
marronne en
caribéenne épicurie.

to allow myself all these positions you say
in mystic cries,
Yé mistikri!
To allow myself all these forbidden positions
and *krik* and *krak*
and *krik krak.*
No, the court will not sleep,
still hand to hand, filled with cries
of hedonistic poetry,
Philosophy,
sweet Philosophy!
I took off
and worse, untamed
and running, I escaped
as a chestnut brown
Caribbean gourmet.

Fantasm fanm

(Creole)

Pou fanm tou sé bèl plézi
Di monté adada osi
« À la Romaine, à l'Andromaque »
Sé pousa ou pé di hak
Sé konsa ou ké kontan
Fè tout sé bagay ou ka di
O pipiri
Tout sé bagay ki intèwdi
An téyori
Kon yo ka di
An fantasm fanm

Sa ki pé rivé nou davré
Di fè tousa ou ka mandé
A sipozé ki nou ka fèy
Dépi nou fè sa épi
Ti bren foli
Puis fanm jodi
Pé ké modi

Mwen ka espéré kou pé konpwann
Sa ki sé kalté pidè fanm
Lè man noz fè
Sa ou ka di-a
Mèm si man sav
Ki fo pa fèy
An jèntifi

54

De bonnfanmi
Kon yo ka di

Atjolman sé mwen ki bandi
Ek sé mwen ké mandé-w li
An mélodi
An narmoni
Kon yo ka di
An fantasm fanm

Es fok tèt an mwen pati
Pou nou pwan titak plézi
An vakabonnajri
Kon yo ka di
An féyéri
An barbari
Pichonnaj ki pa té ka fèt an gran lari
Dousinaj ki nou ka vwè jodi
An pitènri
Kon yo ka di
An frénézi
An malkadi

Pou an fanm sé bèl plézi
Di monté adada osi
Kon sou lérwin Ponpéyi
Alabodaj an bèl péyi
« À l'Andromaque, à la Romaine »
Pa an sèl wozé pijé grènn
An mannyè pakoté Senpyè
An mannyè a lari Lanfè
Fè tout sé bagay intèrwdi
An paradi
Fantasm fanm

Fè tout sé bagay man ka di

An mistik kri
Yé mistikri
Fè krik krak
Kon yo ka di
Yé krak yé kri
An filozofi
Pou lakou pa domi
An poyézi
An malapri
An malfini
Lafilo !
Lavol an pri
Épi kouri
— *Caribéenne*
épicurie —

Urgentes turbulences

à June et Adlai Murdoch

Ô île mienne
Si feu que rien
Love presqu'île tienne
Si tant que bien
S'étend
S'y tend

Que longtemps tiennes
Et tant et tant
Pas comme antan
Esquif esquive en volcanisme

Vénus et Vulcain crachent et crochent
Vénus et Mars cravachent et triment
Prends bons coups de trique

Ogoun Ferraille somme mais consomme
En aporie
En apnée
En empathie *an pati* : je suis partie !

Dure résolument sois parjure
Je t'en adjure
Que toujours dure
L'assentiment !

Urgent Turbulences

for June and Adlai Murdoch

O island of mine
Smaller than a spark
Your peninsula makes love
So much and so well
Extends
Expands

Long may you last
And so much and so much
Not like in bygone days
Skiff evade the volcano's rage

Venus and Vulcan hawk and hook
Venus and Mars whip and overwork
You endure hard hits

Ogoun Ferraille summons but consummates
In aporia
In apnea
In empathy *an pati*: I was transported with pleasure!

Hard resolutely be untrue
I implore you
That our hard-earned assent
Will endure!

Foule
On se défoule
Folle quand t'affole
Frôle mais cajole
Crypte hypocrite
En sondes l'ombrage ombrageux
Mont de Vénus *patat lonbraj* perce
Puis dépèce
Tance somnolences
Exprès expresse
Ta turbulente turgescence

Crowd
Everybody's rowdy
Crazy when I daze
Graze but cajole
Hypocritical crypt
You probe its shy shadows
Mound of Venus *patat lonbraj* drill
Then cut
Rebuke drowsiness
Take care to encrypt
Your turbulent turgescence

De rue d'Enfer à rue Monte au Ciel

Le bougre est descendu à Saint-Pierre,
Martinique, Martinique des cendres,
en février 1902,
a drivaillé en plein Mouillage,
n'y a pas trouvé de daubannes ni nulle dame-jeanne
mais des oeillades de dames Jeanne ad libitum,
s'est fait toiser par la dame
qui a la tête dans les nuages,
le ventre en feu,
le mont de Vénus pelé.
Au pied de la Montagne Pelée,
de rue d'Enfer en bordée
jusqu'à la rue Monte au Ciel
driva de biguine en bordel.
En bord d'eau au fond du Mouillage
et des abyssaux mouillages
goûta des chevelures océanes,
dégusta des rhums et des femmes de toutes couleurs,
visita des ventres de feu,
croisa deux-trois gais zombies
en folle partance
pour de créoles Saturnales,
de fantastiques et voluptueuses chevauchées,
des nuits d'orgie à Saint-Pierre.

A chocolaté
bon enfant,
tout excité,

From Hell's Road to Rise-to-Heaven Street

The fellow went down to Saint-Pierre,
Martinique, Martinique of cinders and ash,
in February 1902,
drifted along for somewhere to moor,
found no Johnny cakes nor demijohns,
only winks from ladies named Jeanne *ad libitum*,
was ogled from head to toe
by the lady lost in the clouds
with fire in her womb,
Venus' bald mound.
At the foot of Mount Pelée,
from the rim of Hell's road
as far as Rise-to-Heaven street,
he was lured by the brothels' beguines.
From the water's shores to the heart
of *Le Mouillage* and its harbor's abyssal depths,
he relished the taste of sea-soaked hair,
feasted on rums and women in all shades and hues,
toured fire-filled wombs,
passed two or three zombies with grins
crazily bound
for Creole Saturnalia,
sultry, fantastic rides,
nights of orgy in Saint-Pierre.

With good will,
aroused,
he groped with chocolate-smeared hands

un lot de diablotins
pierrotins
et de matadors mamelues,
chatouillé des chabines fessues,
une calazaza biscornue,
prodigué suçons et caresses à une capresse à demi nue
au callipyge bonda maté
sans démâter de son côté
jusqu'à ce que sa queue se dévisse,
honoré masques et bergamasques,
masques-la-mort en émoi,
cheval trois-pattes en grand rut,
Marianne la peau-figue alanguie,
vieux-corps vifs à califourchon
en partance pour un Carnaval
de morituri bons vivants,
l'ultime,
le sublime
qui jamais
ne renaîtrait de ses cendres
en telle splendeur bacchanale.

En ce petit temps
court et lourd,
en ce laps d'antan,
en un rien de temps,
à peine à peine
eut-il exonéré ses graines,
songeant à sa légitime
qui l'espérait à Fort-de-France
— poteau mitan
au beau mitan
de l'austérité conjugale —
retira ses pieds juste à temps
pour éviter la Catastrophe.

a crowd of little devils from Saint-Pierre
bedecked with red
and big-breasted matadors, stiletto-heeled,
tickled *chabines* with derrières high and round,
a *calazaza* adorned with a pair of fanciful horns,
lavished caresses and hickeys on a half-naked *capresse,*
a callipyge with buttocks jutting out like masts on a ship,
without cause, for his part, to dismast
until his tail should come undone,
saluted masks and bergamasks,
spirited skeleton brides raised from the dead,
a three-legged horse, crazed in heat,
languid women disguised as Marianne,
men disguised as old bodies astride one another's backs
bound for Carnival
where the *morituri* live well,
the supreme,
the sublime
which never will rise
from cinders and ash
with bacchanal splendor restored.

In this short span of time,
intense and compressed,
in this lapse of bygone days,
a mere nothing of time,
barely, hardly
had he dispersed his seed,
remembering his wife
who was waiting for him in Fort-de-France —
a domestic pillar of strength
in the midst
of wedded restraint —
he retraced his steps just in time
to avoid the Disaster.

Nègzagonale

Elle a débarqué, vent-menée
À l'aéroport du Lamentin
Au bout du petit matin.
Tu l'appelais « chabine calazaza »,
Elle arrivait de l'Autre Bord.
Mamzelle avait été faite là-bas,
Elle avait le teint chocolat
Douci de lait et de miel.

Nègzagonale
Euroblack
Écoute un peu, écoute pour entendre.
Écoute, arrête de faire l'idiot !
Laisse-moi te dire : nous tous, c'est du pareil au même,
Belle petite tôle ondulée cambrée en cadence,
Figure cacao-farine France
Née jusqu'au diable vauvert, 93.
Elle sait juste que sa mère était antillaise,
Elle n'a jamais entendu parler créole.
C'est à Sarcelles qu'elle est allée à l'école.

Négropolitaine, Francoblack,
Écoute un peu, écoute pour entendre.

Il ne faut pas dérespecter la chabine
Parce qu'elle n'a pas bu de toloman,
Pas terroriser cette gamine
Parce qu'elle n'a pas grandi en bas du bois.

Nègzagonale

She landed, windswept
At Lamentin Airport
At the end of the dawn.
You called her "chabine calazaza,"
Newly arrived from the Other Shore.
Mam'selle was born over there,
With a chocolate complexion
Sweetened by honey and milk.

Nègzagonale
Euroblack
Listen a little, listen to learn.
Listen, stop playing the fool!
Let me tell you: it makes no difference to us,
Cute little chassis with rhythmic curves,
Face cocoa-flour from France
Born the devil of a long way from anywhere, department 93,
She only knows her mother was West Indian,
She's never heard a word of Creole.
Sarcelles was where she went to school.

Négropolitaine, Francoblack,
Listen a little, listen to learn.

You must not disrespect the *chabine*
For not having drunk Antillean arrowroot,
Nor fill with terror this gamine
For not having grown in the lower woods.

C'est pas une maquerelle comparaison,
C'est un petit canon jeans et blouson.
C'est pas une choupette,
Lui fais pas sa fête !

Nègzagonale, Euroblack,
Écoute un peu, écoute pour entendre !

Tu l'as surnommée « Mamzelle Poil Mangouste »,
En France c'était une négresse rousse.
Sur l'Autre Bord elle était exotique,
Ici elle est hydroponique.
Où est-elle chez elle ?
Où peut-elle se sentir chez elle ?

Nègzagonale ? Euroblack ?
Négropolitaine ? Plakatak !
Le tambour a résonné, le Carnaval est arrivé,
Le vidé a commencé et elle s'est mise à danser.
Voilà la chabine qui se met à courir le vidé...
Le gros ka l'ébranle, les petits-bois la font onduler,
La musique l'a entraînée.
Voilà Poil Mangouste qui s'est mise à fêter Vaval !
Il n'y a plus de « Nègzagonale ».
Gros ka, ti-bois, pakatak !
Il n'est plus question d'Euroblack,
Le zouk est un zouk d'enfer, une bacchanale !

O Madiana, violons en sac,
Tu ne l'appelles plus « Euroblack »...

Matinino, le jour s'est levé,
C'est toi qui es attrapé !

She's not a shrew spewing lies.
She's a little pistol in jacket and jeans.
She's not a bimbette,
Don't give her a hard time!

Nègzagonale, Euroblack,
Listen a little, listen to learn!

You nicknamed her "Mam'selle With Mongoose Hair"
In France it was red-haired Negress.
On the Other Shore she was exotic.
Here she's hydroponic.
Where is she at home?
Where can she feel at home?

Nègzagonale? Euroblack?
Négropolitaine? Rat-a-tat-tat!

The drum echoes, Carnival here,
She begins to dance as *le vidé*, the procession, hits the streets.
There she goes, the *chabine* who leaps through the parade . . .
The big Ka drum shakes her, mini bamboo drums make her undulate,
Music leads her along.
There she goes, "Mongoose Hair" who welcomes Vaval!
Gone is *Nègzagonale.*
Big Ka, mini drums, rat-a-tat!
No talk of *Euroblack,*
The zouk is a zouk from hell, a bacchanal!

O Madiana, pack up your violins,
You no longer call her "*Euroblack*" . . .

Matinino, day has dawned,
It's you who is caught!

Tu ne la surnommes plus « Poil Mangouste »
Tant elle est belle, tant elle est douce. . .

Laisse-la tranquille, donne-lui de l'air,
Laisse-la un peu faire ses affaires !

Nègzagonale ou Euroblack,
Arrête de draguer ma petite sœur !

You no longer nickname her "Mongoose Hair"
So sweet, so fair . . .

Leave her in peace, give her some air,
Leave her some time to take care of affairs!

Nègzagonale or *Euroblack*,
Stop flirting with my little sister!

Nègzagonal

(Creole)

Manzèl débatjé vanmennen
Laréopò Lamanten
Au bout du petit matin
Ou kriyé'y chabin kalazaza
I té ka rivé lòt bò-a
Ti manzèl-la té fèt lòt-bò
I té ni an ten tjòlòlò

Nègzagonal Euroblak
Kouté pou tann, kouté titak
Kouté, man di'w, pa fè djendjen
Kité mwen di'w : sé menm bagay menm biten
Bèl ti tòl maté an kadans
Fidji kakao farin-Fwans
I né odyabvovè 93
Té jis sav manman'y antiyèz
I pa té ka jen tann kréyòl
Sé Sarsèl i té ay lékòl

Négropoliten Francoblak
Kouté pou tann, kouté titak

Pa dérèspèkté chabin-lan
Pas i pa jan bwè toloman
Pa tèrbolizé ti fi-a
Pas i pa grandi anba bwa
Sé pa an makrèl konparézon

Sé an ti kanon djins èk blouzon
Sé pa an choupèt
Pa fè lafèt !

Nègzagonal Euroblak
Kouté pou tann, kouté titak

Ou kriyé'y Manzèl Pwèl Mangous
Anfwans i té an négrès « rousse »
Lòt bò i té exotik
Isi-a i idroponik
Ki koté kay-li ?
An ki koté i ké kay-li ?

Nègzagonal ? Euroblak ?
Négropoliten ? Plakatak !
Tanbou lévé, Vaval rivé,
Jou rouvè, vidé-a chiré,
Mi chabin-lan voyé monté
Tanbou brennen'y
Tibwa soukwé'y
Mizik-la chayé'y
Mi Pwèl Mangous fété Vaval
Pa té ni pyès Nègzagonal
Pyès Négropoliten isi-a
Gwoka, tibwa
Pakatak, blo !
Pa ni pyès Euroblak ankò
Zouk kraché difé, bakannal
Fini zafè Nègzagonal

O Madiana, vyolon dan sak
Ou sòti kriyé'y Euroblak

Matinino, jou-a ka lévé, ladjé'y !
Aprézan sé ou ki maré

Ou sòti kriyé'y Pwèl Mangous
A fòs i bèl, a fòs i dous

Nègzagonal Euroblak
Kité'y titak, kité'y titak !

Kité'y titak fè zafè'y
Asé zayé ti sè mwen, woy !

CARMINA AMICITIAE

POEMS OF FRIENDSHIP

Odysséenne

à Jacques Fusina

Roulent polyphoniquement ces chants
Sourdent gravement de tréfonds d'îles
S'ourlent jusqu'à ces rivages
Aux abords vagues
Y touchent, se meuvent...
D'un Polyphème courroucé
Se joue l'odysséenne malice
Mais tisse l'industrieuse audace
D'une île à l'autre
Métisse
D'île en île, oui
Par les salvatrices toisons
Crochée aux moiteurs laineuses de l'antre cyclopéen
Cascadant cavalcadant
Chiasmes
Allant encore et voguant de paysage en apaisement
D'idéal en dépaysement
Polyphémique
Du Poète s'étend le carmen
Amoebée le charme s'épand
Sous-tend passerelles par mondes et par mots

Odyssean

for Jacques Fusina

In polyphony these songs roll
Gravely escape from islands' depths
Hem themselves as far as these shores
With ever-changing access
Touch there, flow . . .
Odyssean malice deceives
Polyphemus, incensed
But stitches bold industry
One island to the next
Mestizo
From island to island, yes
By means of life-saving fleece
Crocheted to the cyclopean den's woolly sweat
Cascading, cavalcading
Chiasmi
Going on and drifting from landscape to détente
From ideal to losing one's way
Polyphemean
From the Poet, the *carmen* spreads
Amoebaean singing, the charm pours forth
Undergirds bridges connecting worlds and words

Prosopopée urbaine : Bellevue

aux mânes créoles d'Henri Guédon

Je me nomme Bellevue et je pleure.
Bellevue tambour,
congos,
bongo,
maracas !
Je me nomme Bellevue et je veille,
je me nomme Bellevue et j'accueille
le fruit de mes entrailles,
Henri,
masque yoruba
qui en mon giron planta
l'Arbre de la Liberté.
Je me nomme Bellevue et j'effeuille
partitions et dessins de lui :
synesthésies de pure Beauté.

Urban Prosopopoeia

to the Creole manes of Henri Guédon

I call myself Bellevue and I weep.
Bellevue drums,
congos,
bongo,
maracas!
I call myself Bellevue and I keep watch.
I call myself Bellevue and I receive
the fruit of my womb,
Henri,
yoruba mask
who planted in my breast
the Tree of Liberty.
I call myself Bellevue and I pluck
his designs and musical scores:
synesthesias of sheer Beauty.

Trois points de suspension

aux mânes de Jean-Paul Soïme, Curtis Louisar
et Henri Guédon

Te voici parti, toi aussi ?
Las, nos musiciens amis
S'éclipsent petit à petit

Curtis Louisar, Henri Guédon. . .
Nos amis musiciens s'en vont
Chacun fredonnant sa chanson

Solitaire, sans bruit ni trompette
En priant que ne cesse la Fête. . .
Qu'en nous résonnent à tue-tête

« Aganila », « La Filo », un jazz créole
Un air de guitare ou de viole
— On ne sait — un son qui console

En mélodieux supplément d'âme
Un rythme de biblique anagramme
Un boeuf, un harmonieux programme. . .

Rien d'angoissant ni de morose
« De la musique avant toute chose
Sans rien qui pèse ou qui pose »

Three Times Three Ellipses

to the manes of Jean-Paul Soïme, Curtis Louisar,
and Henri Guédon

Now even you have left, you too?
Alas, our musician friends droop
Little by little slip from view

Curtis Louisar, Henri Guédon . . .
Our musical friends are gone
Each humming his song

Alone, without trumpet or rasp
They beg the Fête to last . . .
Resounding in us at full blast

"Aganila," "La Filo," jazz in Creole
A tune from guitar or viol —
Who knows? — a sound that consoles

With an extra bit of melodious soul
A biblical anagram beat transposed
A riff, a harmonious show . . .

Nothing morose nor filled with distress
"Music above all the rest
With nothing that weighs or remains at rest"

In memoriam Iohannis Claudii

à Jean-Claude Charles

Ferdinand, tu as fui Paris...
Jean-Claude, as-tu suivi Cassegrain, ton lapin Muse et
    confident ?
Tu as marronné vers ailleurs : « Marronner, il faut marronner »,
    dixit Césaire.
Ho, Jean-Claude, ho ! O la ou yé ?
Nous n'irons plus à Barbizon visiter tes amis peintres, saluer les
    mânes de Millet comme nous le fîmes ensemble naguère,
    avec Elvire, espiègle et vive, alors pareille à un elfe en forêt
    de Fontainebleau.
Mais sans doute, dans un bondissement, Cassegrain t'aura-t-
    il mené voir Langston Hughes, Duras, Césaire, Chester
    Himes, ou planer sur l'Artibonite...
Gambader du Marais urbain jusqu'aux abords de réels Champs
    Élyséens où tu te sentiras bien.

In memoriam Iohannis Claudii

for Jean-Claude Charles

Ferdinand, you fled Paris . . .
Jean-Claude, did you tread upon the heels of Cassegrain, your
    rabbit Muse and confidant?
Like a Maroon, you escaped to some other place: "Run away,
    we must run away," *dixit* Césaire.
Ho, Jean-Claude, ho! O la ou yé? Where are you?
We'll no longer call on our painter friends at Barbizon, hail the
    manes of Millet as we did in the past, with Elvire, lively
    and full of pranks, like an elf in Fontainebleau Forest.
Without doubt, in a single leap, Cassegrain will have lead you
    to see Langston Hughes, Duras, Césaire, Chester Himes,
    or to glide over Artibonite . . .
To romp from the urban Marais as far as the outer bounds of
    the true Elysian Fields where you will feel at ease.

Aux cendres de Cendra

à Sandra et Alexandre Cadet-Petit

Ce bougre-là a acheté un briquet, cependant il ne fumait pas.
Cendra, il songeait à Cendra, son éternelle cigarette pointant
au bout de ses longs doigts.

Il a voulu acheter de l'essence avec son petit bidon, pourtant il
n'était pas en panne : la veille il avait fait le plein.
Il était plein de Cendra.
Cendra, il pensait à Cendra et à sa petite Corsa.
Au fond, Cendra, il l'aimait bien.
La Corsa, c'était même lui qui la lui avait payée.
La circulation était dense, lui offrant la possibilité de ressasser...
Il voulut éteindre l'autoradio
Qui le bassinait de chansons d'amour,
De « *Never more* » et de « Toujours »,
Se battit avec les quomodos.
Il n'écouta plus la musique :
« *Man plen épi'y* ! » devint son seul leitmotiv.

La première station était fermée.
Il a eu le temps de réfléchir.
Il n'avait en tête que Cendra.

Il a fait deux stations-service, dans le serein du jour levant,
En a essayé une troisième : c'était ouvert.
Pendant qu'il faisait la queue, il avait encore le loisir de méditer.

To Cendra's Ashes

to Sandra and Alexandre Cadet-Petit

That guy bought a lighter, though he didn't smoke.
Cendra, he was daydreaming of Cendra, her eternal cigarette
    pointing past the tips of her long fingers.

He wanted to buy some gas for his little can, yet he hadn't run
    out: the day before he'd filled the tank.
He was filled with Cendra.
Cendra, he was picturing Cendra and her little Corsa.
Deep down, he liked Cendra quite a bit.
The Corsa — he was the one who had paid for it.
Traffic was heavy, providing him a chance for second thoughts . . .
He wanted the car radio switched off,
Riling him with love songs
Of "Forever" and *"Never more,"*
He fought with the dashboard.
He no longer heard the music:
"Man plen epi'y!" *"I'm fed up with her!"* became his only leitmotif.

The first filling station was closed.
He had time to reflect.
He had only Cendra in his head.

He tried two gas stations, in daybreak's calm.
Then a third: it was open.
He still had plenty of time to meditate, waiting in line.

Cendra occupait ses pensées.

Quand un gars, cigarette brandie, lui a demandé du feu, il l'a
repoussé violemment, a ruminé : « Non, je ne fume pas ».
Le pauvre type lui a répondu : « Tu as raison, fumer tue ».
Cela lui donnait l'occasion de philosopher, ce *bitako* avec son
mégot agrippé à sa portière. . .
Mais il ne l'écouta pas:
Il se concentrait sur Cendra.

Dans la marmelade de voitures, sur l'autoroute,
Au long des longs ralentissements,
Il lui était encore possible de se raisonner.
Il aurait pu rebrousser chemin. . .
Non, il prit des chemins chiens
Pour ne pas rater Cendra.

En la filant jusqu'à la Levée,
Il n'avait à l'esprit qu'une idée :
Nec tecum nec sine te.
Ni avec toi ni sans toi.
En se faufilant jusqu'à l'endroit où Cendra a garé sa Corsa,
Il n'avait d'yeux que pour Cendra.

Quand il a arrosé d'essence la petite voiture,
 — Cendra encore à l'intérieur —
Cendra troquant ses ballerines pour des talons aiguille coquins,
Penchée,
Cendra attachant les petites brides de ses mignons escarpins
sur ses pieds fins,
Consciencieusement,
Cendra, l'être d'élection,
Eut-il une furtive érection ?
Alors il eût pu hésiter : *l'unique* objet de ses pensées, c'était
Cendra.

Cendra invaded his mind.

When a fellow, cigarette brandished, asked for a light, he
    violently shoved him aside, ruminated: "No, I don't smoke."
The poor fool replied: "You're right, smoking kills."
A chance for him to philosophize — this *bitako*, unrefined,
with his cigarette butt, blocking his car door . . .
But he didn't hear,
So concentrated on Cendra.

In the highway's snarl of cars,
In the course of long and lengthy slowdowns,
He could still have used logic.
He could have turned back . . .
No, he took a detour
So as not to miss Cendra.

Tailing her up to the boulevard, la Levée,
Only one idea consumed his brain:
Nec tecum nec sine te.
Neither with you nor without you.
Creeping his way up to the space where Cendra had parked
her Corsa,
He only had eyes for Cendra.

When he had doused her little car with gasoline —
Cendra still inside —
Cendra switching her ballerina flats to saucy stiletto heels,
Leaning over,
Cendra buckling the little straps of her delicate pumps onto
her dainty feet,
Conscientiously,
Cendra, the one elected,
Did he have a furtive erection?
He could have paused: the *sole* object of his thoughts was
Cendra.

Cendra qui ne voulait plus de lui.

Mais quand il a sorti le briquet du fond de sa poche,
Difficultueusement, lentement,
Parce qu'il se prenait dans le tissu,
S'étant palpé tout le corps
Parce qu'il ne se souvenait plus dans quelle poche il l'avait
foutu,
— Sa main trembla-t-elle, alors ? —
Quand il jura
« *Patat'sa* ! »
Quand le briquet neuf s'est enrayé parce qu'il ne savait pas s'en
servir,
Il eut d'interminables secondes pour réfléchir.
Il pouvait encore renoncer.
Pendant qu'il secouait le briquet qui ne voulait pas s'allumer
Parce qu'il n'avait pas l'habitude,
Il a eu le temps de changer d'avis.
Et quand il y a mis le feu, a-t-il croisé son regard ne serait-ce
qu'un fugace instant ?

Combien de temps ce bougre-là l'a-t-il regardée brûler dans
l'habitacle ?
Il était trop tard pour réfléchir,
Mais il pouvait se ressaisir.
En un ultime revirement a-t-il tenté de la secourir,
De la rejoindre dans son embrasement
En un suprême embrassement ?

Cendra, elle s'appelait Cendra.
Lorsqu'il l'a consumée des feux de son faux amour criminel,
a-t-il regardé son visage ?
L'unique *objet* de ses pensées, c'était Cendra :
Réduire en cendres Cendra comme on *réduit* en esclavage.

Cendra who didn't want him anymore.

But when he brought out the lighter from deep in his pocket,
Difficultly, slow as can be —
Because it was caught in the cloth,
Having groped for it, hips to chest
Because he no longer recalled in which pocket it sat —
Did his hand tremble then?
When he swore
"*Patat sa!*" "Dirty whore!"
When the new lighter jammed because he didn't know how to
make it work,
He had endless seconds to reflect.
He could still have renounced his plan.
When he shook the lighter that didn't want to ignite
Because he wasn't adept,
He had time to change his mind.
And when he set the fire, did his eyes meet hers even for one
fleeting instant?

How long did that guy watch her burn in the driver's seat?
It was too late to reflect,
But he still could regain his self-control.
In a last-ditch change of heart, did he try to come to her aid,
Reunite in his raging blaze
In a supreme embrace?

Cendra, her name was Cendra.
When he had consumed her in fires of false criminal love, did
he look at her face?
The only *object* of his thoughts was Cendra:
Reduce Cendra to ashes like one is *reduced* to a slave.

Par mets et par mots

pour Jean-Charles Brédas

Il est un délicieux voyage
À faire par mets et par mots,
Gourmandise pour équipage,
Jean-Charles Brédas aux fourneaux.
Là où coule la Rivière Blanche
S'épand la créolité franche :
Noble est la figure du Chef,
Fier masque d'or d'Agamemnon
Créole, Brédas en son fief
Pas dans l'étroitesse, oh que non !
En belle universalité.
De la haute gastronomie
Jean-Charles est Chevalier, le preux,
Le talentueux maître-queux.
Par une suave synesthésie
Son art met nos sens en émoi :
Des succulences que l'on voit,
Délicatesses que l'on hume,
Nuances subtiles parfument
Et comblent nos papilles en joie.
S'asseoir à la table de Jean-Charles
N'est de ces plaisirs dont on parle
À la légère, mais que l'on goûte
En recueillement, à l'écoute
Du plus raffiné « *Carpe diem* » !
Chef Brédas, c'est pourquoi je t'aime,

By Course and Discourse

for Jean-Charles Brédas

Such a delicious trip
To take by course and discourse,
Gluttony for crew,
Jean-Charles Brédas in the furnace room.
There, where the White River flows,
Our frank Creolity pours forth:
The Chief's face is august,
Agamemnon's proud mask of gold,
Brédas in his fief, Creole,
Not in narrowness — no! —
In beautiful universality.
Of haute cuisine,
Jean-Charles is a Chevalier, heroic
And gifted master cook.
By synesthesia so sweet,
His art makes our senses reel:
Juiciness we see,
Refinement we breathe in,
Subtle nuances perfume
And fill our taste buds with bliss.
To feast on one of Jean-Charles's meals
Is not a joy of which we speak
Lightly, but rather we enjoy
In reverence, tuned in
To the most refined "Carpe diem!"
Chef Brédas, this is why I love you,

Toi qui, en officier de bouche
Rendant un novateur hommage
Au matrimonial héritage
De nos *potomitan* d'antan
— Femmes debout et *grands-manmans* —
Flattant d'un coulis de passion
Le goût d'un foie gras, d'un poisson,
Sais concocter tant de délices,
Pour créer par exquises touches
En féerique dévotion,
Jubilatoire célébration,
La fête des saveurs métisses.

Master-at-arms of the mouth,
Who pays innovative hommage
To matrimonial heritage
Of our *potomitan* of days gone by —
Grands-manmans and upright wives —
From a coulis of passion fruit, arousing
The taste of foie gras, of fish,
You know how to concoct so many delights
To design with a delicate touch
In devotion worthy of myth,
Celebration with no end,
The fête of flavors of mixed descent.

LACONIQUE ART
POÉTIQUE

LACONIC *ARS POETICA*

Canons étonnants et tonnant

pour Peter Klaus de la Freie Universität Berlin
et May Livory de Barde la Lézarde,
« pastille », ou plutôt « j'ai lu le . . . » poétique

Blogodo ! Voilà que tonnent
Soudain les canons étonnants
Des littératures francophones
À Berlin, en docte symposium
En grand paintingue, en grande pompe.
Devrais-je être dans mes petits souliers
Pour éviter de débarquer
Là-bas avec mes gros sabots
De petite marronne insulaire ?
Gare à ne pas faire la bitako,
Quasimodo, grosso modo
En ce cénacle universitaire
Où, trompeuses, sonnent et claironnent
Les trompettes de la renommée,
Où se mettent en perce ces mystères
D'iniquité.
Hors de question que je détone
Ou que je détonne.
Woy papa'y ! Voilà que résonnent
Vieux canons et perspectives! . . .
Manman ! Voilà qu'on raisonne :
Grands dieux ! Sont-elles mortes ou vives
Nos Belles-Lettres francophones ?
Pour ma part je ne m'en soucie guère.

Astounding Canons Resounding

for Peter Klaus from the Free University of Berlin,
and May Livory of Barde la Lézarde,
a "pastille," or rather a poetic "j'ai lu le . . . "

Blogodo! Boom! All of a sudden astounding
Canons of francophone literary works
Of art resound
In Berlin, in a learned symposium
En grand paintingue, so solemn, with great pomp.
Would I have to watch my step
When I land over there
To avoid getting off on the wrong foot,
A little Maroon islander?
Beware of playing the *bitako*, gross,
Quasimodo, *grosso modo*
In this academic inner sanctum
Where false trumpets of great renown
Ring out and sound,
Where iniquity's secrets
Are broached.
Out of the question for me to detonate, go off
Or go off key.
Woy papa'y! Ooh la la! All of a sudden
Old canons and new perspectives resound! . . .
Manman! Sweet mother of god! All of a sudden they reason:
Good heavens! Are they dead or alive
Our francophone belles-lettres?
As for me, I hardly care.

Il est grand temps que je marronne.
Ni maîtres ni métropoles
Ni Dette de sale fric
Pour l'Afrique
Ni règles ni normes
Ni *Code Noir* ou blanc
Mais marron
Ni lois pour atteindre l'Idéal
Ni canons tonnant
Ne m'étonnent.

It's high time that I escape like a runaway slave.
Neither masters nor metropoles
Nor dirty money's Debt
For Africa
Nor rules nor norms
Nor *Code Noir* black or white
But maroon
Nor laws to achieve the Ideal
Nor resounding canons
For me are astounding.

CLAUSULE

CLAUSULA

Juste un changement inchangé

Tout est désormais bien plus simple, même le fait d'être
compliqué,
Métis, hybride, sang mêlé : c'est juste un changement inchangé
Puisque le temps n'existe pas.
Puisqu'aussi bien
Insensiblement s'abolit
Du temps l'infini servage,
S'en abolit l'esclavage.
Le temps n'est pas un ennemi, oui !
Juste un changement inchangé
En une Abolition sereine
Où être pareillement mélangé
Hic et nunc se met à faire sens.
En Abolition souveraine
On cesse de croire en des rengaines
Frelatées ; fini de fredonner des fredaines
Annihilantes,
Aliénantes.
À force de n'être ni tout l'un
Ni tout l'autre,
Voilà qu'on commence et finit
Par être le Tout, le grand Tout, l'omnitendanciel.
Qu'en ce bas monde s'élève enfin
Cette algébrique équation,
Cette latine syntaxe qui stipule
Que plusieurs négations s'annulent !
En résultera, germinale, l'immémoriale affirmation
Liminaire sauvegardant tout, fors les stigmates,

Just an Unchanging Change

Henceforth all is much simpler, even the fact of being complex,
Métis, hybrid, mixed blood: it's just an unchanging change
Since time does not exist.
Since equally well,
Imperceptibly, little by little, the infinite serfdom of time
Becomes extinct,
So, too, slavery.
Time is not an enemy, yes!
Just an unchanging change
In serene Abolition
Where being mixed in the same way
Hic et nunc, here and now, begins to make sense.
In sovereign Abolition
We stop having faith in the same old refrains
Full of hype; let's finish humming crazy pranks —
Annihilating,
Enslaving.
By not being all of the one
Nor all of the other,
We achieve the be-all and end-all
Of being the All, the great All, the *Omnitendentious*.
From this lower world
May this algebraic equation ascend at last,
This Latin syntax that states
That several negations annul themselves!
As a result, affirmation of old,
Proemial, germinal, safeguarding all, except for scars,
Timeless acceptance of self and the Other

L'intemporelle approbation de soi et de l'Autre
En sempiternel devenir :
C'est le vieux nègre qui joue au *sèbi*,
Le poing stigmatisé de fers.
Aujourd'hui c'est le jeune bougre aussi,
Le poumon oppressé par de pesantes chaînes d'or
Et les doigts s'accrochant, mystiques,
À une chevalière colossale en une incantation bossale
Conjurant tous les mauvais sorts et pseudo-malédictions.
Comme en temps de fête patronale,
Comme antan sur la plantation
En temps de répit,
En terre urbaine aujourd'hui
Du temps s'abolit l'esclavage
Car la relève est assurée :
C'est juste un changement inchangé.
C'est bien au *sèbi* que ça se joue :
Ensorcelant le jet de dés
Tout un chacun serre dans sa main
Sa liasse de billets bien lissés
Qui finissent bien pliés en quatre, vitement lancés
Sur le carré de feutrine verte, d'une poigne preste,
Soumis aux caprices des *zo* sommés de faire sept
Ou onze au hasard de leurs facettes,
Insoumis au cicatriciel partage des eaux,
Aux relents nébuleux de la Traite.
Ces dés — *zo* de leur nom créole,
Car le vieux nègre naguère se les taillait dans des os —
En un magico-religieux lié au jeu,
Subjugué,
Hors du joug d'antan c'est le jeune bougre
Qui d'une dextre experte désormais va les expulser du gobelet,
Insoucieux du joug mémoriel.
De la main gauche sans cesse il remonte son ceinturon,
La moitié des fesses à l'air, son derrière rebondi tendant le
coton fleuri de son caleçon

In a state of eternal evolving change:
It's the old Negro who rolls the *sèbi*, the dice,
Fist branded by iron chains.
Today it's the young fellow as well,
Chest oppressed by heavy golden chains,
And mystic fingers that cling
To a giant signet ring in an African magic chant
Warding off all bad luck and pseudo-curses.
As in days of feasts for patron saints,
As in bygone plantation days
In times of reprieve,
In urban land today
Our enslavement by time is repealed
For relief is assured:
It's just an unchanging change.
It's well played out with *sèbi*:
Casting spells on each throw of the dice
Everyone clasps in his hand
His wad of well-smoothed bills
That end up folded in fours, quickly tossed
On the green felt square with a nimble command,
Subjected to whims of *zo*, bones, summoned to add up to
seven,
Or, chance willing, facets creating eleven,
Refusing to bend to cicatricial dividing of waves,
To the vague stench of slave trade.
These dice — *zo* by their Creole name,
For the old Negro, some time ago, carved them from bones —
In a magical-piety tied to the game,
Subjugated,
Out of the yoke of former days, it's the young man
Who henceforth, by means of a skillful right hand, will eject
them from the shaker,
Unmindful of memory's yoke.
With his left hand, he constantly pulls up his belt,
Half of his buttocks exposed, his bouncing behind stretching

Qui déborde du *baggy* taille basse d'où dépassent deux chevilles malingres
Hors du jean gigantesque exprès.
Tournent et tourbillonnent les dés.
C'est au tour du vieux corps de jouer
En ce moment même comme antan
En ces temps nouveaux mais pareils
Avec le zouk pour tonitruante mélodie
Tel un bel air d'aujourd'hui, de jour
Comme par la lune claire naguère.
C'est une suave palinodie,
Juste un changement inchangé.
Combien de fois te fut-il donné de sursauter
À chaque « *Sizan* » invoquée comme une déesse propitiatoire
En cri de victoire et d'espoir
Par celui qui a fait un providentiel six ?
Tout est devenu bien plus simple,
Même le fait d'être compliqué,
Métis, chabin ou *chapé* :
C'est juste un changement inchangé.

the flowery cotton of boxer shorts
That protrude from the baggy low waist, and two puny ankles are seen
Emerging from huge, over-sized jeans.
The dice revolve and reel.
It's the old body's turn to play
In this exact moment like former days
In these new times but the same
With the zouk for booming strains
Like the *bel air* beguine of today, in the sun
As under the clear moon some time ago.
It's a sweet palinode,
Just an unchanging change.
How many times were you given a jolt
At each "*Sizan*" invoked like a goddess to bring luck
With each victory whoop or cry of hope
By the one who made a six, heaven-sent?
All has become much simpler,
Even the fact of being complex,
Métis, chabin or *chapé*:
It's just an unchanging change.

POET'S NOTES

"Pointe-des-Nègres," "Aux horizons du Sud," "In Southern Horizons," and "Moun le sid"
Pointe-des-Nègres : quartier de Fort-de-France, lieu de débarquement des esclaves déportés d'Afrique pendant la traite négrière.
(Pointe-des-Nègres is the quarter in Fort-de-France where slaves, deported from Africa during the slave trade era, came ashore.)

"Nègzagonale"
En 1991, en citant « Au bout du petit matin » — leitmotiv du Cahier *d'un retour au pays natal — j'ignorais que l'aéroport du Lamentin se nommerait « Aéroport Aimé Césaire » en 2008. Il n'y a pas de coïncidences, il n'y a que des correspondances.*
(In 1991, quoting "at the end of the dawn" — which is a leitmotif in Aimé Césaire's *Cahier d'un retour au pays natal* — I didn't know that in 2008 Lamentin Airport would be called "Aimé Césaire Airport." There are no coincidences; there are only correspondences.)

"Prosopopée urbaine : Bellevue" / "Urban Prosopopoeia"
Bellevue : quartier de Fort-de-France où vécut Henri Guédon.
(Bellevue is the quarter or district in Fort-de-France where Henri Guédon lived.)

"Canons étonnants et tonnant" / "Astounding Canons Resounding"

La « pastille » est une prescription de May Livory, un médicament poétique qui finit et commence par le même phonème à la rime; moi, vu la forme oblongue de mon poème, j'ai plutôt fait une « gélule »: une « j'ai lu le . . . ».

(A "pastille" is a prescription from May Livory, a poetic drug that finishes and starts with the same rhyming sound; seeing the oblong form of my poem, instead I've made a "gélule": a "j'ai lu le . . .")

TRANSLATOR'S NOTES

Punctuation and formatting:
In accordance with French conventions, in the original French and in the Creole versions of Suzanne Dracius's poems we have retained European-style quotation marks and also spaces prior to colons, question marks, exclamation points, and other terminal punctuation marks.

"Propitious Anamnesis"
The number 93 (*Neuf Cube*) designates a run-down area in the suburbs of Paris, whose postal code begins with this number. Wordplay involves the two meanings of *neuf* ("nine" and "new") as well as the two meanings of "cube" ("block," and "cubed" in the mathematical sense). *Métissage* refers to the blending of two distinct elements, in either a biological or cultural sense. *Chabin* is a term used to describe a biracial man with red or blond hair and some black features. *Marronnage* refers to the flight of slaves from their masters. *Rebeu* or *beur* (meaning an Arab) and *sefran* (meaning a French person) are French slang words constructed by reversing syllables. *Périf* is an abbreviation for "périphérique": the boulevard périphérique is a 36-kilometer ring road around the French capital, dividing Paris *intra muros* from the surrounding suburban *banlieues*.

"Subnigra sum sed formosa"

Ravet is the Creole word for "cockroach." In French, *avoir le cafard* means to have the blues (there is no equivalent in Creole).

"Pointe-des-Nègres"

Fongo, Dankan, Goanuà, Nchi Kavu, Goà, Souf, Terrou-bi, Lessdi, Mabélé, Oto, Monkili, Hmsé and *Molongo* are words from various African languages that mean "land" as seen from the sea, when one arrives by boat. The word *Tchip!* represents a loud sound made by sucking one's teeth with one's tongue, familiar in most black cultures, including those from the Caribbean, Africa, or United States; this sound usually communicates disapproval.

"Terres-Sainville"

This prosopopeia is spoken in the voice of Terres-Sainville. *Zorey* is a Creole word used to describe a white French person originally from France, not Martinique.

"In Southern Horizons"

Quimbois is an Afro-Caribbean, Creolized form of witchcraft and healing practices, often involving herbal potions. The name comes from the Creole word *Tjenbwa* and is built on the injunction *Tiens bois*, which means "Take this and drink." *Banania*, a French cocoa-flavored breakfast powder, originated in 1912, using ingredients imported from France's tropical colonies. *Bique, bicot, crouille,* and *melon* are offensive words used to describe North African Arabs living in France. *Keubla* (meaning "black") is a pejorative French slang word constructed by reversing syllables.

"Antonomasia in Cyclone Times"

"DS 21" refers to the initials of "Dracius, Suzanne," born on August 21, during the cyclone season. This also refers to the Citroen DS 21, a popular car during the poet's school years and a nickname given to her by classmates. The Homeric "hapax" referenced is "Dracius" (*Iliad*, 13, 692), which later became one of the surnames assigned to newly freed slaves in Martinique in the mid-nineteenth century. "Suicard," a French-sounding name, is "Dracius" spelled backwards. "The Pleiades" refers to a group of sixteenth-century French poets who espoused the revolutionary goal of ennobling the French language by imitating ancient Greek and Roman literature.

"Haruspicy at Century's End"
In ancient Rome, haruspices were religious officials trained to interpret omens by inspecting the entrails of sacrificial animals. The Romans also ascribed meaning to the direction in which birds took flight. *Kalmisiré* is a Creole word meaning *calme et cirée* (calm and waxed). *Ad vitam aeternam* is Latin for "to eternal life."

"Women's Fantasies"
"Hell's Road" refers to *rue d'Enfer*, the name of a street in Saint-Pierre, Martinique, which was destroyed by the volcanic eruption of Mount Pelée in 1902. "Rise-to-Heaven Street" refers to *rue Monte au ciel*, which is nearby. *Krik krak* is part of a Caribbean storyteller's ritual of warming up the audience by asking "*Krik?*" and encouraging the collective response "*Krak!*" The storyteller then says, "*Yé mistikri!*" and the audience responds, "*Yé mistikra!*" Then the storyteller will ask, "Is the court sleeping?" and the audience responds, "No, the court is not sleeping."

"From Hell's Road to Rise-To-Heaven Street"
References in this poem to the finely calibrated racial distinctions on the black/white continuum found in Martinique include *calazaza* (light-skinned mulatto woman with red or blond hair and very few black features), *chabine* (light-skinned biracial woman with red or blond hair and some black features), and *capresse* (half-black, half-mulatto woman with darker skin than the *chabine*'s, and with black hair). *Marianne la peau-figue* refers

to a major Carnival caricature dressed in dry banana leaves; *figue* is the Creole word for banana, and Marianne represents the fruit's fragility.

"Nègzagonale"

Nègzagonale and *nègropolitaine* are pejorative French names used to describe West Indians born in France, combining *nègre* with *hexagonale* (referring to the hexagonal shape of France) and *metropolitaine* (also pertaining to France); "Euroblack" and "Francoblack" are synonyms for these terms. *Madiana* and *Matinino* are old Amerindian names for Martinique. "O Madiana" is the name of a traditional Creole song sung at the end of a festive ball.

"Odyssean"

Odysseus, who wandered ten years before finding his way back to his homeland, is used here as a metaphor for biracial experience. Polyphemus was a one-eyed Cyclops who trapped Odysseus and his companions in a cave; after blinding Polyphemus in his eye, they escaped by tying themselves to the undersides of Polyphemus's sheep. In Latin, the word *carmen* means "song," "tune," or "poem."

"Urban Prosopopoeia"

The word "manes" refers to the tutelary spirits of the dead. Henri Guédon was a Martiniquan percussionist, painter, and sculptor who died after heart surgery on February 12, 2006, in Paris, France.

"Three Times Three Ellipses"

Jean-Paul Soïme (who died on August 9, 2007) was a Martiniquan violinist, composer, and author whose group Malavoi performed the song "La Filo." *Soïme* is an anagram for *Moïse* (Moses). Curtis Louisar (who died in April 2007) was a Martiniquan singer and guitarist who wrote the song "Aganila." Henri Guédon (who died in February 2006) was a Martiniquan percussionist, painter, and sculptor. The last two lines of this poem come from Verlaine's "Art poétique."

"In memoriam Iohannis Claudii"

The title of this poem is Latin for "In Memory of Jean-Claude." Jean-Claude Charles (1949–2008) was a gifted and well-published Haitian writer known for his errant lifestyle, living in such places as Mexico, Chicago, New York, and Paris. Ferdinand and Cassegrain are characters featured in his last novel, *Ferdinand, je suis à Paris* (*Ferdinand, I am in Paris*). Elvire is Charles's daughter.

"To Cendra's Ashes"

On June 12, 2005, Sandra Cadet-Petit, a secretary who worked in the mayor's office in Fort-de-France in Martinique, was burned alive in her car by her ex-boyfriend. Robert Mariello was only sentenced to twenty years of prison, with the opportunity for parole after thirteen years, because the jury did not find him guilty of premeditated murder. This poem was inspired by Dracius's belief that the crime was indeed premeditated. She changed the name "Sandra" to "Cendra" to evoke the French word "cendres," meaning "ashes," as well as to represent all women who are victimized by domestic violence. May 22, the date when this poem was completed, is a holiday that commemorates the abolition of slavery in Martinique.

"By Course and Discourse"

Jean-Charles Brédas is an award-winning chef from Martinique, whose creations combine ingredients from cuisines around the world. *Potomitan* is the Creole word for "pillars of strength," and *grands-manmans* is Creole for "grandmas."

"Astounding Canons Resounding"

"J'ai lu le . . . " (I've read the . . .) is pronounced the same as "gélule" (pill in the shape of a capsule): this is wordplay in French.

"Just an Unchanging Change"
Sizan is the Creole word for "Suzanne" and is part of an expression shouted out each time a dice player throws a six. *Chapé* is a Creole word with a pejorative connotation, used to describe a biracial man.

ACKNOWLEDGMENTS

Translation of this work was supported in part by funding from the government of Montgomery County, Maryland, and the Arts and Humanities Council of Montgomery County. Additional funding for the production and publication of the book was received from the National Endowment for the Arts. All sources of support are deeply appreciated.

Poems from the collection previously appeared in the following journals.

The Caribbean Writer: "The Gap of the Cracked-Open Door" and "Just an Unchanging Change"

Circumference: "From Hell's Road to Rise-to-Heaven Street"

Colorado Review: "Three Times Three Ellipses"

Connotation Press: An Online Artifact: "*Subnigra sum sed formosa*," "Urban Prosopopoeia," and "Urgent Turbulences"

Cordite Poetry Review: "*In memoriam Iohannis Claudii*" and "Terres-Sainville"

International Poetry Review: "Propitious Anamnesis"

The Iowa Review: "Nègzagonale"

Little Patuxent Review: "Pointe-des-Nègres" (nominated for a 2013 Pushcart prize)

Loch Raven Review: "To Cendra's Ashes"

Mantis: "Astounding Canons Resounding"

Notre Dame Review: "Antonomasia"

Prairie Schooner: "By Course and Discourse"

The Sligo Journal: "In Southern Horizons"

Subtropics: "Odyssean"

Weave: "Haruspicy at Century's End"

Words Without Borders: "Women's Fantasies"

Other books from Tupelo Press

Fasting for Ramadan: Notes from a Spiritual Practice (memoir), Kazim Ali
Another English: Anglophone Poems from Around the World (anthology),
    edited by Catherine Barnett and Tiphanie Yanique
Pulp Sonnets (poems, with drawings by Amin Mansour), Tony Barnstone
Moonbook and Sunbook (poems), Willis Barnstone
Pulp Sonnets (graphic poetry); Tony Barnstone and Amin Mansouri
gentlessness (poems), Dan Beachy-Quick
Living Wages (poems), Michael Chitwood
Or, Gone (poems), Deborah Flanagan
The Posthumous Affair (novel), James Friel
Entwined: Three Lyric Sequences (poems), Carol Frost
Poverty Creek Journal (lyric memoir), Thomas Gardner
the good dark (poems), Annie Guthrie
The Faulkes Chronicle (novel), David Huddle
Darktown Follies (poems), Amaud Jamaul Johnson
Dancing in Odessa (poems), Ilya Kaminsky
A God in the House: Poets Talk About Faith (interviews),
    edited by Ilya Kaminsky and Katherine Towler
After Urgency (poems), Rusty Morrison
Lucky Fish (poems), Aimee Nezhukumatathil
The Infant Scholar (poems), Kathy Nilsson
Weston's Unsent Letters to Modotti (poems), Chad Parmenter
Mistaking Each Other for Ghosts (poems), Lawrence Raab
Intimate: An American Family Photo Album (hybrid memoir),
    Paisley Rekdal
Thrill-Bent (novel), Jan Richman
The Book of Stones and Angels (poems), Harold Schweizer
Cream of Kohlrabi (stories), Floyd Skloot
The Well Speaks of Its Own Poison (poems), Maggie Smith
The Perfect Life (lyric essays), Peter Stitt
Soldier On (poems), Gale Marie Thompson
Swallowing the Sea (essays), Lee Upton
Butch Geography (poems), Stacey Waite
Lantern Puzzle (poems), Ye Chun

See our complete list at www.tupelopress.org